The Science of SUPERPOWERS

Jennifer Kroll, M.A.T., Ph.D.

Consultants

Timothy Rasinski, Ph.D.
Kent State University

Lori Oczkus
Literacy Consultant

Publishing Credits

Rachelle Cracchiolo, M.S.Ed., *Publisher*
Conni Medina, M.A.Ed., *Managing Editor*
Dona Herweck Rice, *Series Developer*
Emily R. Smith, M.A.Ed., *Content Director*
Stephanie Bernard and Susan Daddis, *Editors*
Robin Erickson, *Multimedia Designer*

Image Credits: Cover illustration by Timothy J. Bradley; p.9 Tehsigo Eternamente (J Mondragon)/Flickr; p.10 Mikkel Juul Jensen/Science Source; pp.12-21 comic illustration by Travis Hanson; pp.24–25 Walt Disney/Courtesy Everett Collection/Alamy Stock Photo; pp.32–33 Marvel Studios/AF Archive/Alamy Stock Photo; pp.34–35 Stephen Dalton/Science Source; p.37 Science Source; p.38 SPUTNIK/Alamy Stock Photo; p.45 John Devries/Science Source; p.52 Jim Zipp/Science Source; All other images iStock and/or Shutterstock.

Teacher Created Materials
5301 Oceanus Drive
Huntington Beach, CA 92649-1030
http://www.tcmpub.com

ISBN 978-1-4938-3608-6

Printed in Malaysia.
Thumbprints.45293

Table of Contents

Superheroes and Science

Superheroes have thrilled readers for decades. The first superhero comics appeared in print before the start of World War II. Today, graphic novels about superheroes still fly off library shelves. Kids, teens, and adults flock to theaters to watch these heroes save the day. Spider-Man! Batman! Avengers! We can't seem to get enough of superhero stories. And it's no wonder. These fun fictions are chock-full of action, suspense, good, evil, and … *science?*

Elements of a Superhero

Superhero storywriters like to make up imaginary metals and other **elements**. The Marvel® character Wolverine has claws and bones that are coated with "adamantium." Wonder Woman's bracelets are made from "amazonium." Captain America's shield is made with "vibranium."

A Form of Sci-Fi

Superheroes and science? Sure! With gamma rays, black holes, and mutants, superhero stories are full of ideas borrowed from science. These stories imagine what the technology of the future may be like. Story characters own and use amazing vehicles, weapons, and gadgets. They travel through space and time. With so many science and technology elements, superhero fiction is really a form of **science fiction**.

A Super Alien

Science fiction stories sometimes tell of beings from other planets. The comic book hero Superman is from the planet Krypton. He travels to Earth as a baby.

Mad Scientists and Mighty Mutants

He's testing out his new freeze ray. He's laughing as he pours smoking liquid into beakers. His evil experiments turn people into mutants. Who is this **sinister** character lurking in the lab? It's a mad scientist, of course! And it will take a superhero—or maybe a team of rebel mutants—to stop this kind of evil genius.

Brains vs. Brawn

The Ultra-Humanite was an early mad-scientist supervillain. He first appeared in a 1939 Superman comic. He was Superman's opposite. He had a weak and crippled body but a brilliant, evil mind.

Scientists Gone Bad

Mad scientists appear in many superhero stories. These characters crave power, and they want knowledge. They don't care who gets hurt along the way. One of Spider-Man's biggest enemies is a mad scientist named Dr. Otto Octavius. "Doc Ock" has mechanical tentacles attached to his body. In the Batman stories, the hero must face off against Mr. Freeze. This villain was once a scientist who worked with frozen bodies in a **cryogenics** lab. He suffered a lab accident and now must wear a refrigerated suit. He seeks revenge on Batman, whom he blames for his misfortunes.

THINK LINK

- Mad scientists in stories sometimes go too far with their experiments. How might a science experiment "go too far"?
- What kinds of experiments are controversial in society right now?
- Who should have the power to decide what types of scientific experiments are okay and not okay?

Mighty Mutants

Some superheroes—and super villains—are mutants. These characters have special abilities that no ordinary human could have. The members of the X-Men are all mutants. Wolverine has the ability to heal rapidly. Jean Grey has telepathic and telekinetic powers. She can read thoughts and move objects with her mind. Storm is a mutant who can control the weather.

The stories about these mighty mutants are pure fiction. Yet the concept of mutants comes from the world of science. The cells of living things contain something called DNA, and it is DNA that determines how organisms will look and act. Parents pass DNA to offspring. Each DNA strand is made up of genes. When a gene or group of genes changes from what has been normal in the past, this is called a **mutation**. The changed organism is sometimes called a *mutant*.

In some superhero stories, an accident causes a character's mutation. A character gets exposed to powerful rays or chemicals. This is how Dr. Bruce Banner becomes the Hulk. Some mutants are created by the military or by scientists. In Marvel Comics, cosmic beings called the Celestials give some people special "X-genes." The people born with these genes have mutant superpowers.

A Magnetic Personality

Magneto is a mutant character who can create and control magnetic fields. Is it possible for a human to have this power? Scientists don't think so. But some people have claimed to be human magnets like Magneto.

From Pets to Ninjas

The Teenage Mutant Ninja Turtles have been kid favorites for decades. The heroes began as ordinary pet turtles. Then, they were exposed to radiation and mutated into human-like forms.

Raphael and Michelangelo

Meet Some Real Mutants

You'll never meet a superhuman mutant like Storm or Wolverine in real life. Teenage Mutant Ninja Turtles won't emerge from your city's sewers. But there are some mutations that really happen. The following mutations are all real.

Albino Animals

Albinos lack the gene for melanin, the **pigment** that gives skin and hair its color. Albino animals are white and have pink eyes. Albinism is a common mutation that occurs in nature. People can have this mutation, too.

Glow-in-the-Dark Felines

Did you know there are cats that actually glow? Scientists have changed the cats' DNA as part of an experiment. The cats were given a gene from a fluorescent jellyfish. This was to help scientists study a virus in cats that mimics HIV. The ultimate goal of the experiment is to help them find a way to cure the deadly AIDS virus.

A Web-Slinging Goat

This might look like an ordinary goat, but scientists at Utah State University have changed this animal's DNA. The scientists added a spider gene. Now the goat produces a spider's dragline silk in its milk. Scientists believe that the super-strong spider silk could have medical uses. It might some day be used to help repair torn **ligaments**.

Hidden Genes

Two non-albino parents can produce offspring with albinism. This can only happen, though, if both parents are "carriers" of the trait. The diagram to the right shows how it can happen.

STOP! THINK...

- How many of the children shown on the diagram above are carriers for albinism?
- If these parents had eight children, how many might be carriers for albinism? How do you know?

The Science of Super Strength

Many comic book heroes and villains share at least one superpower: super strength. How do these characters get to be so strong? The stories vary. Some superheroes, such as Iron Man, get their strength from specially designed armor. In some stories, scientists set out to transform an ordinary person into a super-strong being. The scientists might be working for a villain or as part of some secret military program.

Imagine that you are part of a team of scientists—good or evil. You have been given the task of designing a super-strong superhuman. How might you go about this task? Where would you get your inspiration and ideas? Perhaps you might look to the animal world …

Animal Inspiration

Some superheroes and villains take their names from animals. They have qualities and capabilities associated with the animals they're named after.

A grizzly bear is one of the strongest animals I can think of.
I watched one topple a garbage dumpster once, and the bear rolled that huge dumpster repeatedly as if it were playing with a beach ball!
A grizzly bear must be considerably stronger than a human to be able to do that. Hmmm. We will have to study bears further, Doctor.
Did you know that a bear's bone strength doesn't diminish during hibernation?
Yes, we should be able to learn a great deal about strength from examining bears.
And some species of bears hibernate for more than seven months at a time.

The Biggest of Bears

Polar bears are even larger and stronger than grizzlies. An adult male polar bear can weigh 1,500 pounds (680 kilograms), 600 pounds (272 kilograms) more than an adult male grizzly!

Mighty Muscles

Scientists at NASA are trying to unlock the secrets of how bears' muscles and bones stay so strong during hibernation. They hope to use what they learn to help astronauts cope better with the lack of gravity in space travel.

A grizzly bear is an amazingly strong animal, Doctor, but it can't lift 50 times its own body weight. There isn't any animal that can do that, is there?
We ... actually you're looking at another amazing animal capable of such a feat.
I am?
A leafcutter ant, like the one you see here, can easily hoist and carry an object weighing 50 times more than its body weight. That makes such a creature, in a way, stronger than a grizzly bear—considerably stronger.
50x
An ant stronger than a grizzly bear? That seems absurd.

Mighty Mouths

An ant does its heavy lifting with its mandibles, not its legs. Mandibles are appendages attached to an insect's mouth—like giant jaws. An ant uses mandibles to cut up its food, defend itself, and carry items.

Ant-spiration

In the Ant-Man comic, scientist Hank Pym discovers a chemical that can change a person's size. He ends up shrinking himself down to just half an inch (1.27 cm) tall!

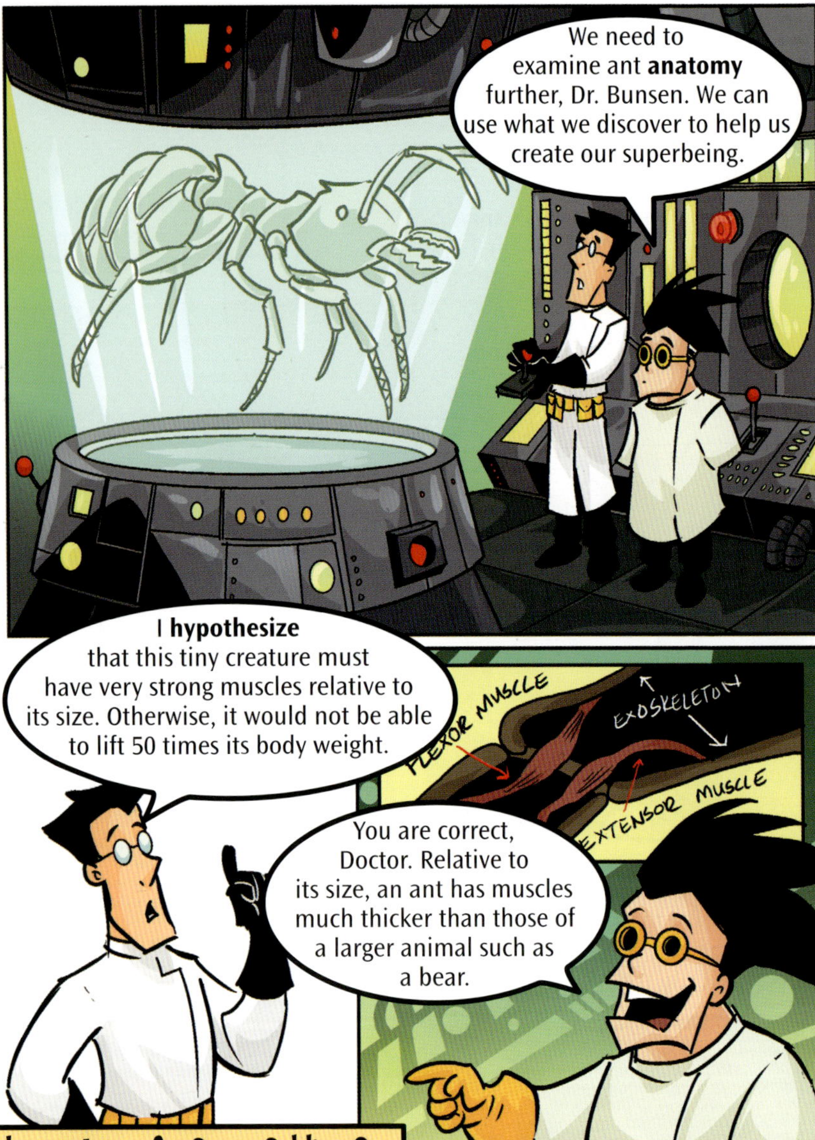

Insect Armor for Super Soldiers?

One company is developing a robotic suit for the United States military. The exoskeleton suit, called the XOS®, will allow a human who wears it to lift hundreds of pounds. The suit also increases the wearer's agility.

An ant doesn't have bones like a bear, either. An ant has a much lighter—but stable and strong—**exoskeleton**. A bear uses a great deal of energy just lifting its own heavy bones and limbs.
An ant, on the other hand, is very lightweight and doesn't have to expend so much energy lifting itself. That's why it can lift 50 times its body weight.
We have learned valuable information from studying these insects!
Meet the Beetles
Ants aren't even the strongest animals on the planet in terms of relative strength. That title goes to the dung beetle. A dung beetle can pull over 1,000 times its own body weight.

Animal anatomy is fascinating, and it can be a source of many useful ideas.
I have another idea. Let's give our creation the über-grip of an eagle.
An excellent thought! An eagle's talons can grab and hold its prey at a strength of 2,600 pounds per square inch (464 kilograms per centimeter). That's like having nails that can cut through concrete.
Or perhaps, we could design our superbeing's arms to mimic the strong tentacles of a giant squid.

A Real Dr. Octopus?

Spider-Man's **nemesis**, Doc Ock, has robotic octopus tentacles fused to his body. Could robotic tentacles really be attached to human bodies? Maybe. Robotic **prosthetic** limbs are already real.

DIG DEEPER!

Can Super Stress Give You Super Strength?

Grrr! Dr. Banner becomes the Incredible Hulk when he feels threatened and angry. Can real people develop super strength when they are under super stress? Could a panicking dad lift a car off a baby? Could an ordinary woman fight off an attacking polar bear? Stories about such incredible feats of "hysterical strength" abound. Many of them are probably not true. Even so, scientists do know how and why stress and fear make humans faster, stronger, and more able to withstand pain. Here's what happens in the body when a person experiences an intense threat.

When threatened, a primitive part of the brain called the *amygdala* takes over. The brain stops all unnecessary thoughts. It focuses all energy on the threat.
The mouth gets dry from lack of saliva.
The heart pounds to deliver extra blood to the muscles.
Pain-deadening chemicals flood the brain.
The body loses its ability to focus on small motor tasks (like writing or drawing).
Digestion stops, as do other body processes not related to fight or flight.
A hormone called *cortisol* surges through the body. It releases sugar into the bloodstream to feed muscles.
The body's strength increases.
The body is able to react more quickly than normal.

Superpowers: From Fiction to Fact

Superpowers don't exist in the real world. Or do they?

Surprise! Some of the abilities of your favorite superheroes are—or might soon be—possible in real life. Scientists and inventors are at work right now on technology that could turn these superpowers from fiction to fact.

Now You See Her . . .

Susan "Sue" Storm Richards is also known as the Invisible Woman. She is a member of Marvel's Fantastic Four. This superhero can make herself vanish. She can also make objects invisible. Sue uses her mental powers to bend the wavelengths of light around herself or around objects. This creates the illusion of invisibility.

Sue isn't the only superhero who can disappear. The Green Lantern, Space Ghost, Iron Man, and the Hood are among those who share this talent. Unlike Sue Storm, some superheroes use special clothes or gear to vanish. Iron Man's stealth armor lets him become invisible. The Hood uses an invisibility cloak.

Making a TV Disappearance

Claude Rains is a character on the superhero TV miniseries *Heroes*. He has the ability to vanish.

Invisible and Incredible

Violet Parr is a character in the Disney•Pixar animated film *The Incredibles*, which is a movie that spoofs superhero tales. Violet has the power of invisibility.

Invisibility—A Possibility?

Of course, vanishing superheroes aren't real. They are just fiction. But scientists are working on ways to make invisibility a future reality. They have already built tiny cloaks that make microscopic objects seem to disappear!

Abracadabra in the Lab

Researchers at the University of California, Berkeley, designed a tiny invisibility cloak. The cloak is made from thin layers of silicon oxide and silicon nitride on a silver mirror. The researchers have tested their invention, and it works!

How do they work? The cloaks are made from **metamaterials**. These are ordinary materials that are shaped in special ways. For example, one team of scientists is using gold to mold metamaterials. Another team is working with ceramics. The scientists work to shape the materials so that light bounces off them. When a cloak is placed in front of something, people cannot see the object. They might see the space behind the objects. Or they might see nothing at all.

Right now, scientists can only cloak tiny and unmoving objects. Invisibility suits for humans may not be available for many years. But the research is underway. Invisibility is looking more and more possible!

THINK LINK

- What would be some of the possible uses of invisibility technology?
- What kind of problems might occur if invisibility cloaks were widely available?
- Would you want to have the superpower of invisibility? Why or why not?

A Force-Field Shield

Sue Storm has more than one superpower. In addition to being able to vanish, she can also create force fields. She can place invisible protective shields around herself or other people or objects. She generates force fields by using her special mental powers.

Other superhero and villain characters also create and use force fields. These super-powered characters include Jean Grey, the Silver Surfer, and Magneto.

Force-Field Facts

Magnets are very strong objects that can be used for many different things. In fact, scientists use powerful magnets to produce force fields. And you thought magnets were only for decorating your locker and refrigerator!

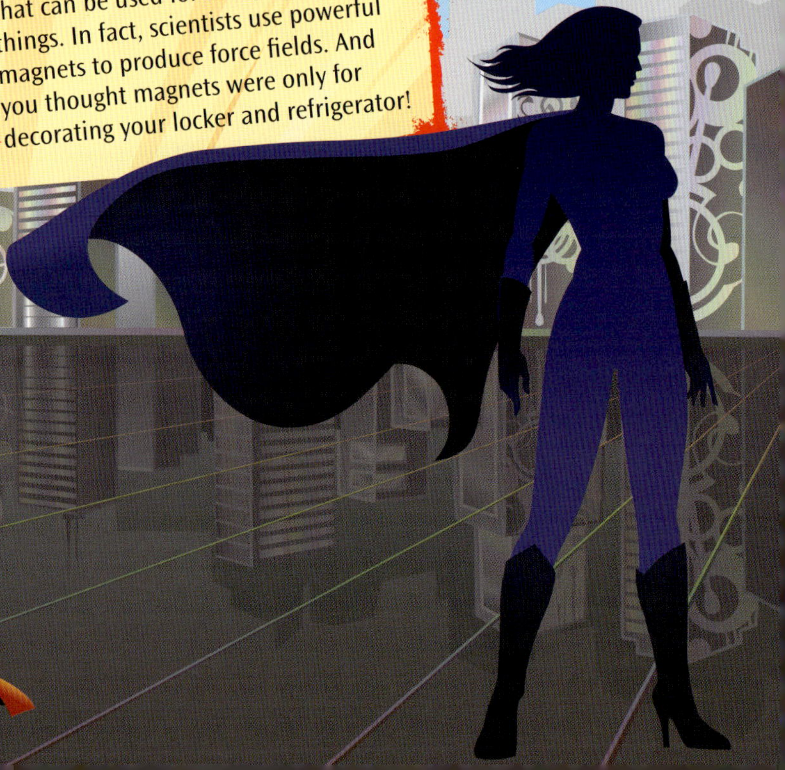

Are force fields fictional like the characters that use them? They might seem like the stuff of science fiction, but force-field technology is taking off. An aircraft company has a **patent** on a force-field system. The system uses an **electromagnetic** arc to repel shock waves from explosions. The arc is not quite like the force field of a superhero. It cannot repel solid objects such as bullets. But this kind of force field could still save lives. It may soon be used to help protect military vehicles.

Safer in Space

NASA is working to develop magnetic force-field technology. The technology will help protect spacecraft from deadly solar radiation.

An Amazing Aqua-bility

Wouldn't it be cool to breathe underwater? The DC Comics™ superhero Aquaman has this superpower. Aquaman needs no oxygen tank or scuba suit to dive down into the ocean's depths. He can stay **submersed** as long as he wants—just like a fish.

Do you ever wish you could spend time hanging out with sea creatures? Does the thought of tankless diving fill you with aqua envy? If the answer to these questions is yes—good news! Scientists at the University of South Denmark have developed a **crystalline** substance that could make it possible for humans to breathe underwater. The sponge-like substance, nicknamed the "Aquaman crystal," is made from **cobalt**. The crystal can absorb and store oxygen, drawing it out of air or water. The oxygen can then be released when heat is applied to the crystal.

The Aquaman crystal has not yet been developed into a form that divers can use, but it may someday make oxygen tanks unnecessary. That would not only be great for divers—it could also help patients with lung problems. Right now, patients with severe lung problems are sometimes hooked up to oxygen tanks. Aquaman crystals would free them in many ways.

Another Water Wonder

Aquaman isn't the only superhero character that can breathe underwater. Namor the Sub-Mariner is a Marvel character that shares this talent.

Antiheroes Who Heal

Wolverine is a fierce, yet fascinating, character from a series of comic books as well as movies. Wolverine is not a classic superhero. He is an **antihero**. But he still has impressive superpowers! He has sharp **retractable** claws. He has keen animal-like senses. He has great agility and strength, too.

Wolverine has something more as well. He has what is called a "healing factor." He can recover with superhuman speed from illness or injury. Serious injuries that would be fatal to others still hurt him but are not deadly.

Another Marvel character with this same ability is Deadpool. He is a complicated character. Deadpool is a mix of good and evil. But he can do something that Wolverine cannot. Deadpool can regrow a lost limb or organ!

Regrowing a limb sounds impossible. But is it?

A Price for Power

Many characters pay terrible prices for their amazing abilities. Characters often experience intense suffering. This is usually a result of their abilities. For some, super abilities can equal super pain.

Welcoming a New Wolverine

A comic series titled *All-New Wolverine* features a female version of the iconic character. The female Wolverine has super-healing powers, just like the male original.

Amazing Healing Animals

Limb regrowth may not be as impossible as it sounds. Certain kinds of animals can **regenerate** lost or damaged parts. A flatworm cut in half will regrow into two healthy flatworms. Sea stars can regenerate lost arms. The axolotl is another animal with this superpower-like ability. Axolotls are Mexican salamanders that can regenerate lost body parts.

Not Leaving the Lake

Axolotls are **neotenic**. That means that they keep juvenile traits into adulthood. Axolotls never grow lungs. This is unlike other salamanders. They don't leave the water to live on land, as most amphibians do. Scientists believe there is a connection between the neotenic nature of these animals and their healing capabilities.

How do animals such as axolotls regrow lost limbs? Why don't humans share this ability, and would it be possible for people to develop it? Researchers at the Children's Hospital in Boston recently stumbled onto a clue when conducting cancer research on mice. The mice were divided into different groups. The researchers clipped holes in the ears of the mice in one group. They did it to identify the mice. But the ears kept healing.

The researchers tried again. They needed a way to keep track of the mice. They clipped the tip of a toe off each mouse. But the toes grew back to normal, too. What was happening?

Sit! Stay! Heal!

Though they can't regrow lost limbs, dogs are animals with healing powers. They produce a special protein in their saliva that helps their wounds heal quickly.

The mice in the regrowth group had certain altered genes. One of these was a gene called Lin28a. This gene is active during the early development of mice as well as humans. It gives an unborn baby the ability to regenerate damaged **tissue**. It allows young mice—or humans—to recover quickly from injuries. Later in life, this gene gets "switched off." The organism's ability to regenerate limbs and heal rapidly goes away. Researchers realized why the mice in the research were healing so well. Their Lin28a gene had been changed. It had remained "switched on."

Scientists are left wondering if the discovery of the gene's power could make it possible for humans to regrow limbs. Perhaps future generations will have superhero-like healing powers. It's possible, given what scientists have already learned. What seems like super fiction today may one day be super reality.

Don't Try This at Home!

It should go without saying, but you should not try to replicate any experiment or steps described in this book.

Meet Thomas Hunt Morgan

This super scientist won a Nobel Prize in 1933. He discovered much about how genes and **heredity** work. He was fascinated by the regenerative powers of certain animals.

Sea One, Sea Them All

The sea cucumber is another amazing animal with regenerative powers. When one is cut into pieces, a new sea cucumber will grow from each piece.

A Real Life Spider-Man

On June 1, 2007, people strolling down the sidewalk near the Jin Mao Tower in Shanghai, China, looked up and got a surprise. A man in a Spider-Man suit could be seen clinging to the side of the tower. The people stopped and gawked as the hooded figure climbed higher and higher. Could Spider-Man be real? Was a superhero scaling the city's tallest building? Or was it a madman up there, 1,200 feet (366 meters) in the air?

Alain Robert climbing the Federation Tower in Moscow, Russia

The man in the Spider-Man suit was Alain Robert, a French stunt climber. Some people might argue that Robert is indeed mad. He has climbed skyscrapers and landmarks in cities all around the world. He climbed the Eiffel Tower. He scaled the Sydney Opera House. He topped the New York Times Building. He even ascended the tallest building in the world, the Burj Khalifa Tower in Dubai. In 2011, Robert set a record. He climbed the 985-foot (300 meter) Aspire Tower in Qatar in the fastest time ever. He set the record—one hour, 33 minutes, and 47 seconds—a few months before his 49th birthday.

Spidey's Origin

The fictional Spider-Man, teen Peter Parker, receives his wall-climbing ability and "spider-sense" that alerts him to oncoming threats after being bitten by a radioactive (or genetically altered) spider.

Nature's Climbers

Human beings can climb, but they are not as well adapted for this activity as some other creatures are. Spiders, squirrels, monkeys, and geckos are among the creatures best adapted to climbing.

Without a Web

Unlike the fictional Spider-Man, Alain Robert possesses no special spider skills. He sometimes uses ropes and wears a safety harness. But many of his urban climbs have been completed without ropes, harnesses, or webs. Often, the only special gear Robert uses is climbing shoes or sticky tape for his fingertips. Tied to his waist, he carries chalk, which he uses to help keep his hands from slipping. These "free solo" climbs are incredibly dangerous. One false move while high up on a skyscraper will almost certainly result in the stunt climber's death.

A Common Fear

Some people love to climb. But many people suffer from the fear of heights, called **acrophobia**. Some scientists think this may be a natural fear that humans have for protective reasons.

It may be hard to understand why Alain Robert does it. He says that he has always simply loved the exhilarating feeling he gets from climbing. He enjoys setting new climbing challenges for himself. As a child, Robert loved to climb trees near his home. As a teenager, he became very involved in the sport of rock climbing.

Super Spiders

Spiders have a number of capabilities that seem almost super. Not only can spiders climb walls and spin webs, but they can also regenerate a lost or broken leg. And spiders can see ultraviolet light, which means they can see colors that humans cannot.

A Rocky Start

Although he is an experienced climber, Alain Robert took some very serious falls early in his career. At 20 years old, he fell about 50 feet (15 meters) after an anchor that held his rope gave way. This fall resulted in a wrist broken in five places, a broken ankle, a broken knee, and a broken nose. A headfirst fall six months later put Robert in a coma for five days. That fall shattered his forearms and fractured his skull. Robert would later suffer a second nearly fatal fall. After awakening from another coma with numerous broken bones, he spent two months in a hospital. Doctors told him he was lucky to be alive. But he had suffered about a 60% loss of ability in his hands and arms. In fact, this caused him to be considered permanently disabled.

Talented Tails

Some animals are specially adapted for climbing. These animals often also have adaptations to help them survive falls and escape injury. Animals such as geckos and squirrels use their tails to help them land in upright positions.

Caution!

Climbing is extremely dangerous. Even experienced, professional climbers need to be careful. If you want to start climbing, be sure to never climb without proper training and protective gear. To challenge yourself in a safe way, visit a climbing gym or adventure ropes course. And always follow safety rules carefully.

Amazingly, Robert was determined to climb again. He recounts in his autobiography, *With Bare Hands*, how he recovered his strength and agility. He did it by climbing across a brick wall near his home. At first, Robert could only move across two or three bricks without falling off the wall. After about two months, he could cover an arm's length of the wall. Eventually, he could make his way down the whole wall.

Urban Climber

Alain Robert had never planned to climb a building. Then one day, a film director called him. The director was making a **documentary** about climbing. He wanted to film Robert climbing a cliff in Utah. He also wanted film footage of a climber scaling a Chicago skyscraper. Robert agreed to be part of the project.

Getting the city footage turned out to be difficult. Most building owners understandably do not want stunt climbers scaling their buildings. And police do not want people to put themselves at risk in this way. But Robert did end up climbing a Chicago skyscraper.

A Safety Line for Spiders

Spiders use lines of silk in the same way that human climbers use safety lines. If a spider gets into trouble, it can crawl up the line to safety.

Since then, Robert has climbed buildings all over the world. That is how he earned nicknames such as "The French Spider-Man" and "The Human Spider." Robert seems to embrace these nicknames. He has even climbed several buildings in a Spider-Man costume. In 2004, he climbed in costume to promote the premiere of a Spider-Man movie on a TV station.

Batman's Line Launcher

Batman can't cast a line of spider silk like Spider-Man does. But he can use the line launcher gadget on his utility belt to make a zip line or a tightrope. Bat-tastic!

DIG DEEPER!

A Feat of the Feet (or Legs!)

One way that stunt climber Alain Robert trains is by crawling around on the ceiling of a room in his home. He has installed handles on the ceiling so that he can work out daily in this way. Robert's ability to crawl on the ceiling is impressive not only because it showcases how well he has overcome major injuries but also because, despite his nicknames, Robert is no comic book hero with superpowers.

It takes a lot of effort, strength, and skill for human beings to crawl across ceilings. Spiders, by contrast, can do this almost effortlessly. How do spiders walk up walls and across ceilings so easily? Scientists think they might know.

- Spiders have hairs on their legs.
- They also have very tiny hairs on the hairs. These smaller hairs are called **setules**.
- An attraction between the **molecules** in the setules and molecules on the surface of the ceiling makes the spider stick.

Stickier Sticky Notes

Product designers can use what scientists have learned about spider legs to make better products. They could, for instance, use the knowledge to design stickier self-sticking notes.

Going Gecko

Geckos, like spiders, can climb walls effortlessly. Scientists at Stanford University recently created a "synthetic adhesion system" inspired by the mechanics of gecko feet. The handheld device allows a person to climb by sticking to walls!

Up, Up, and Away!

What ability do Superman, Supergirl, Iron Man, the Silver Surfer, and the Green Lantern have in common? These superheroes all have the power of flight. Human beings have long dreamed of being able to leap into the air and go "up, up, and away." In fact, independent flight might be the most desired of all superpowers. Looking to nature—as well as to fiction—we can see the many reasons why flight is such a "must-have" superhero skill.

A Norse Flying Horse

The gods of many ancient cultures were imagined as being able to fly. In Norse mythology, the god Odin flies through the air on a horse. The flying horse, named Sleipner, has eight legs.

A Superpower for the Ages

Gods. Angels. Fairies. Stories of flying beings have been told for thousands of years. Over and over in the tales and myths of many cultures, we see fantasies of flight. Today, air travel is an everyday reality. Planes allow us to fly around the world. We can go sightseeing in a helicopter or spend a Saturday learning to hang glide. Yet we still can't leap into the air and simply fly off, superhero style. As in ages past, we are left to envy animals and fictional heroes who possess this superpower.

Wings of Wax

The Greek myth of Daedalus and Icarus reflects humanity's longing for flight. This father and son fly with wings made of feathers and wax. Icarus soars too close to the sun, and its heat melts the wax, causing him to plunge into the sea.

As the Crow Flies

Ever hear the expression *making a beeline*? How about *as the crow flies*? Such expressions reflect the fact that winged animals have a serious advantage when it comes to travel. They can get where they need to go more quickly and directly than ground animals can. Honeybees can travel up to 15 miles (24 kilometers) per hour. Many birds, such as crows, can fly four times that fast. Some bird species are even faster, like the frigate bird, which can soar at speeds of 95 miles (153 kilometers) per hour. That leaves even the fastest ground animal, the cheetah, in the dust.

Eagle Eyes

An eagle is able to spot a small animal, such as a rabbit, from two miles (3.22 kilometers) away. It has much sharper eyesight than a human does.

So when it comes to helping a superhero get to the right place fast, the power of flight has no equal. Instead of sitting in traffic or racing through a maze of city streets, a high-flying hero can get right to the scene of the crime. And flight also gives the hero a bird's-eye view of everything he or she needs to see to get the job done.

Batman Takes Off

Despite his name, Batman doesn't have the power to fly like a bat. He does, however, have flying vehicles and devices that allow independent flight.

Hawk Heroes

Hawkman and Hawkgirl are DC Comics superheroes. They have hawk-like powers, including the power to fly.

Fight and Flight

What's that swooping out of the sky? Is it a bird? Is it a plane?

Well, actually, yes. It *is* a bird. It's a peregrine falcon, the fastest bird on Earth. A peregrine falcon can reach speeds of 200 miles (322 kilometers) per hour while diving for prey. This mighty hunter swoops in so fast that its prey has little time to escape. The falcon's super flight powers give it something important—the element of surprise.

peregrine falcon

Soaring with a Surfboard

The Silver Surfer is a superhero who can fly not just in Earth's atmosphere but also into outer space. He travels on a craft that looks like a surfboard.

Flying superheroes can similarly use the element of surprise to their advantage. Imagine the Green Lantern diving down to take out Sinestro. Imagine Superman suddenly swooping onto the scene to save the floundering Justice League. Surprise, villains!

And the power of flight isn't only advantageous when a superhero is on the attack. Flying also provides a means of near instant escape. When Iron Man is dodging the Mandarin's lethal rays or Supergirl's ice breath fails to freeze the villain, these superheroes can still soar to safety.

STOP! THINK...

Two hundred teenagers were surveyed. The teens were asked which superpower they would prefer to have: flight, speed, or invisibility.

- Which superpower was most popular?
- Why might teens like that power the best?

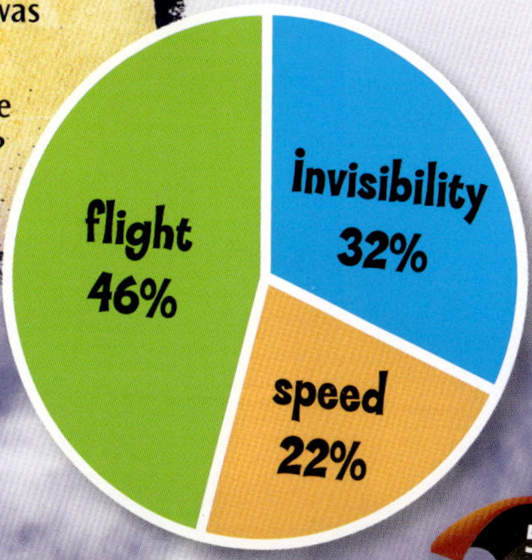

Simulating Flight

Independent flight would certainly be one of the most useful superpowers, but it would also be super cool! The whole world would suddenly be open to you.

Perhaps that's why flight is a key superhero power. Comic books are filled with flying heroes. But when those superheroes are depicted in film, what do the actors do? Even the best actor can't act his or her way into taking off in flight!

Big Business

Superhero movies are big business in Hollywood, and they have been since *The Mark of Zorro* was made in 1920. How big? *The Avengers* made about 1.5 billion dollars worldwide in 2012.

Where Are My Rocket Boots?

Superheroes such as Iron Man fly with help from technology, such as Tony Stark's rocket boots. In real life, working jet packs and rocket boots have existed for decades. However, such devices require a lot of fuel and can only store a limited amount of fuel at a time. This means that only very brief flights are currently possible.

The earliest films simulated flight with hidden ropes and wires. Wind machines blew the "flying" actors so that it looked as though the heroes were flying through the sky. In time, "green screens" were used. Actors moved in various ways, filmed against a chroma key composite, or green screen. The green was later replaced with a filmed shot—for example, a span across building tops. Suddenly, it appears that the actor is actually flying across those buildings!

Today, CGI—or computer-generated imagery—is used. This special technology makes it seem as though anything is possible. If you can think it, CGI can create it.

Where Fantasy Meets Fact

Superhero stories take us out of our own lives and into exciting worlds. They are worlds populated by heroes and villains with extraordinary talents. Flying. Wall crawling. Super strength. Healing factors. All these superpowers and the characters who possess them are products of the imagination. Yet the stories of these superhumans contain many ideas borrowed from the world of science. Mixed in with elements of fantasy, we find kernels of fact.

A Super Future?

We can also maybe—just maybe—see possibilities for the future. What if fictional superpowers someday become real? We might live in a world populated by mutants—good and evil—with amazing abilities. Do you think technology such as force fields, rocket boots, or super armor would make the world a better place? One day, these impossible dreams may become our reality. And what if you had the chance to develop a superpower? Would you want the action-packed, **turbulent** life of a superhero? Or would you rather just put your feet up and enjoy reading a great graphic novel or comic book *about* your favorite superhero?

Sci-Fi to Fact

Science-fiction writers of the past have predicted many technologies of the present. Writer Arthur C. Clarke predicted the existence of communication satellites. Ray Bradbury imagined earbuds in his famous novel *Fahrenheit 451*, published in 1953.

Your Own Superhero

Imagine you are a writer, a cartoonist, or an animator. You wish to create a new superhero. What kind of superpowers would you give your character? Why?

Glossary

absolute strength—the total amount of force that an organism can exert

acrophobia—the fear of heights

anatomy—the physical structure of a plant or animal

antihero—a leading character in a story who lacks certain heroic qualities, such as honor and nobility

cobalt—a silver-white metallic element

cryogenics (kry-uh-JEN-iks)—the study of what happens to organisms at very low temperatures

crystalline—like a crystal; clear and transparent

documentary—a movie or television program that gives factual information

dormant—asleep or in a state of inactivity

electromagnetic—having qualities of electricity and magnetism

elements—substances which cannot be broken down into simpler substances

exoskeleton—a hard external covering on an animal such as an insect or crustacean

heredity—the passing of traits from one generation to another

hormone—a substance formed inside a body that affects functions of the body

hypothesize—to make an educated guess that can be tested

ligaments—membranes that support organs of the body and keep them in place

metamaterials—materials that are engineered in complex, heavily structured ways, allowing them to have properties not typically found in nature

mutation—a sudden change in an organism caused by a change in a gene or a chromosome

nemesis—worst enemy

neotenic—demonstrating the ability to hold onto traits normally only seen in juveniles, or children

patent—the rights to make, use, or sell a certain invention

pigment—a natural substance that gives color

prosthetic—a device that substitutes for a missing part of the body

regenerate—to re-create, renew, or regrow

relative strength—the strength of an organism in relation to its size

retractable—able to shrink back or be withdrawn

science fiction—a type of fiction that draws imaginatively on scientific knowledge or predicts the future

setules—small hairs on the hairs of spider legs

sinister—looking threatening or evil

submersed—positioned underwater

tissue—a group of cells that together form a part of an organism

turbulent—disturbed; in a state of disorder

Index

Check It Out!

Books

Alain, Robert. 2010. *With Bare Hands: The True Story of Alain Robert, the Real-life Spiderman*. Blacksmith Books.

Enz, Tammy, and Agniezka Biskup. 2014. *Batman Science: The Real-World Science Behind Batman's Gear*. Capstone Young Readers.

Kakalios, James. 2009. *The Physics of Superheroes: Spectacular Second Edtion*. Avery.

Sandvold, Lynnette Brent, and Barbara Bakowski. 2009. *Superhero Science: Kapow! Comic Book Crimes Fighters Put Physics to the Test*. Gareth Stevens.

Solomons, David. 2015. *My Brother Is a Superhero*. Viking Books for Young Readers.

Videos

PBS. 2013. *Superheroes: A Never-Ending Battle*. DVD.

Websites

DC Comics. http://www.dccomics.com/.

Marvel. http://www.marvel.com/.

Try It!

Just like some of the scientists and superheroes in this book, you are going to help save the world! Several pages in the book reference plants, animals, and bugs that are used to create helpful products for humans. You've been hired by a biotech company to come up with an environmentally based invention to help others.

- First, what societal problem do you want to solve? It can be local, national, or worldwide.
- Look around at your surroundings. What plant or animal has special physical qualities to help you accomplish your goals?
- Draw a diagram or blueprint of your prototype. Include labels and captions explaining each part of your new invention.
- You should also include an explanation of the problem you are solving, why it's important to you, and how you came up with your idea.
- To take it to the next level, how could you actually build the prototype if you have the means and supplies available?

About the Author

Jennifer Kroll owns a cape, but, unfortunately, she is not a superhero. If she could have only one superpower, she would choose to have a "healing factor," like Wolverine. However, she would also really like to be able to fly. Kroll is the former senior editor of Weekly Reader's *Read* magazine and the author of 15 books for kids, teens, and teachers. She enjoys researching and writing about science topics and is currently working on her first science fiction novel. She lives in Connecticut with her super husband and two super kids.